MW01601213

I'm a Blessing Magnet

Stirring Up Faith to Expect God's

Goodness Every Day

e

Dr. Steve Mbua

I'm a Blessing Magnet

ISBN: 979-8-9904267-4-0

Copyright at 2025 by Dr. Steve Mbua

Invest in the Gospel at:

- Wesbite: https://www.cityrevive.org/give/
- Cash App: https://cash.app/$ciicus
- Paypal: https://www.paypal.com/paypalme/ciicdonate
- Thank you for your generosity. Please make checks payable to CRC and mail your gift to: 17701 FM 2115, Salado, TX 76571
- If you want to become a Partner with our ministry, email: pa@cityrevive.org or go@cityrevive.org

Table of Contents

Introduction

Have you ever paused to wonder what your life could look like if you truly believed that blessings were drawn to you?

Too often, we live with a scarcity mindset—hoping, wishing, and striving for God's goodness while quietly doubting if it's really for us. But what if I told you that you were never meant to chase blessings? You were born to attract them.

I'm a Blessing Magnet is not just another inspirational book. It's a faith activation. Within these pages, you'll discover how to live each day expecting God's favor, speaking His promises, and aligning your life with His abundant plan. This book is your invitation to stop striving and start receiving.

Whether you're walking through lack, believing for breakthrough, or simply hungry for more, this journey will reframe how you think, speak, and receive.

You are a magnet for miracles. Let's stir up your faith—and live like it.

—Dr. Steve Mbua

Born to Be Blessed

Chapter 1

Born to Be Blessed

"Then God blessed them, and God said to them, 'Be fruitful and multiply; fill the earth and subdue it...'"
— Genesis 1:28 (NKJV)

Man was never meant to live a life of lack, fear, or frustration. From the very beginning of creation, the first words God ever spoke over humanity were words of blessing. Before God gave Adam and Eve a task, He empowered them: "Be fruitful."

That blessing wasn't just poetic—it was prophetic. It carried divine power to prosper, increase, and rule. That same blessing is your spiritual inheritance in Christ.

What Does "Blessing" Really Mean?

To say, "I'm a blessing magnet," you must understand what a blessing really is.

The Hebrew word "Bārak" means to bless, empower, bestow favor, to speak divine increase over someone.

So, when God blessed Adam and Eve, He wasn't just giving them good wishes. He was releasing heavenly power into their lives to multiply and rule.

Greek (New Testament):

In the Greek language the word blessing is "Eulogía." It means a good word, a gift of benefit, divine favor spoken and released.

Just like a "eulogy" speaks well of someone, this word blessing means God speaks well of you—and His Word carries transforming power with the ability to change your current state of living into a blessing magnet.

"Blessed be the God and Father of our Lord Jesus Christ, who has blessed us with every spiritual blessing in the heavenly places in Christ." — Ephesians 1:3

You're not trying to get blessed—you already are that's what the Word says.

You Carry a Blessing Identity

The world might have labeled you unworthy, unlucky, or forgotten. But God calls you blessed and highly favored.

"Christ has redeemed us from the curse of the law… that the blessing of Abraham might come upon the Gentiles in Christ Jesus…" — Galatians 3:13–14

Because of Jesus, you now walk in the same blessing Abraham received: a covenant of increase,

What Is a Magnet? (Spiritually Speaking)

A magnet pulls certain objects toward itself by an invisible force. In the same way, when your heart is full of faith, you begin to attract God's favor and goodness. Faith creates a spiritual magnetic field.

"Be it unto you according to your faith."

— Matthew 9:29

When you believe, expect, and speak in agreement with God's Word, you pull blessings into your life. Your faith is not passive—it's a magnetic force that draws the invisible into the visible.

Abraham the Blessing Magnet

One of the most powerful examples of a "blessing magnet" in the Bible is Abraham. Abraham was indeed a blessing magnet in every sense of the word. His life demonstrates how faith and obedience to God can attract unimaginable favor, influence, spiritual and material legacy.

Here are a few key reasons Abraham was a blessing magnet:1. God's Promise Made Him a Magnet

"I will make you into a great nation, and I will bless you; I will make your name great, and you will be a blessing."

— Genesis 12:2 (NIV)

5

God didn't just bless Abraham — He made him a source of blessing. Abraham became a spiritual and natural magnet for divine favor because he carried a divine promise.

2. His Faith Pulled Blessings to Him

"Abram believed the Lord, and he credited it to him as righteousness."

— Genesis 15:6 (NIV)

Abraham's faith was like a spiritual magnet. He trusted God when there was no visible proof, and display of that kind of faith drew the supernatural into his life — including wealth, protection, and generational influence.

3. His Obedience Activated the Blessing Flow

"By faith Abraham, when called… obeyed and went, even though he did not know where he was going.

— Hebrews 11:8 (NIV)

Obedience was the key that unlocked the blessing. He followed God's voice without a map, and in doing so, he entered into a land of divine provision.

4. Even Others Were Blessed Through Him

"...and all peoples on earth will be blessed through you."

— Genesis 12:3 (NIV)

Abraham's blessing overflowed — his life magnetized blessing not only for himself but for nations and generations after him. You could say he carried a blessing anointing that was contagious.

5. He Attracted Wealth, Favor, and Protection

- Pharaoh gave him riches (Genesis 12:16).
- Kings respected him.
- His enemies feared him (Genesis 14).
- Even Lot was blessed by association.

Everywhere Abraham went, he prospered — not by striving, but by believing he wasn't chasing blessings — blessings were chasing him.

And through Christ, that same Abrahamic blessing rests on you:

"If you belong to Christ, then you are Abraham's seed, and heirs according to the promise."

— Galatians 3:29 (NIV)

Joseph the Blessing Magnet

Another powerful example of a "blessing magnet" is Joseph. Betrayed by his brothers, sold into slavery, falsely imprisoned—yet through it all, he prospered.

"The Lord was with Joseph, and he was a successful man..." — Genesis 39:2

Joseph didn't have ideal conditions. But what he had was the presence and blessing of God. That blessing promoted him in Potiphar's house, preserved him in prison, and ultimately elevated him to lead all of Egypt.

"The Lord was with him; and whatever he did, the Lord made it prosper."

— Genesis 39:23

Joseph didn't chase promotion—promotion chased him. That's the power of the blessing. And the same blessing is now yours through Christ!

It's Okay to Expect Good Things

Some people believe expecting blessings is prideful or greedy. But God loves when His children believe Him for more. Expectation is the heartbeat of faith.

"Surely goodness and mercy shall follow me all the days of my life..."

— Psalm 23:6

You don't have to beg for blessings. You are a child of the King. Goodness follows you. Favor finds you. Breakthrough belongs to you.

Say it boldly:

"I am a blessing magnet!"

Prayer:

Heavenly Father,

Thank You for blessing me through Jesus Christ. Open my eyes to see Your goodness already working in my life. Teach me to expect, declare, and walk in Your promises every day. Let the same blessing that was on Abraham and Joseph rest on me and my household. From this day forward, I choose to believe that I am a magnet for Your miracles, favor, provision, and peace. In the name of Jesus, Amen.

Personal Reflection:

1. Have I been living more aware of burdens or blessings lately?

2. What areas of my life do I want to start expecting God's blessings in?

3. What's one declaration I can speak daily to stir my faith?

Prophetic Confession:

"Father God, I thank You that blessings are not far away from me. They are chasing me. I receive them today by faith…"

What You Expect,
You Attract

Chapter 2

What You Expect, You Attract

Faith Is Magnetic

"Now faith is the substance of things hoped for, the evidence of things not seen." — Hebrews 11:1

What you expect in life matters. In fact, your expectation sets the boundaries for your experience. You will never rise higher than your faith allows. If you expect defeat, you attract discouragement. But if you expect blessing, you attract breakthrough.

Expectation is the heartbeat of faith. And faith is the magnet that draws the supernatural into your everyday life.

Faith Is the Magnet for Miracles

Miracles are not random. They're not just for the "super spiritual." They are the natural outcome of faith placed in a supernatural God.

Faith pulls on the invisible realm of heaven and draws it into your visible life. That's why Jesus often responded to miracles not by saying, "I did this," but by saying, "Your faith has made you well."

Faith is a spiritual magnet—it attracts healing, favor, open doors, wisdom, provision, and divine intervention.

"Without faith it is impossible to please God…"

— Hebrews 11:6

Why? Because faith pleases God to move. He's already willing—but it's your faith that positions you to receive.

Think of it this way:

1. Doubt repels.

2. Fear delays.

3. Faith attracts.

Jesus didn't say, "According to My power let it be to you." He said,

"According to your faith let it be to you."

— Matthew 9:29

That means your miracle isn't waiting on God—it's waiting on your faith-filled expectation. The stronger the magnet of your faith, the more it pulls on heaven.

Examples of Faith as a Magnet in Scripture

Throughout the Gospels, people who received miracles all had one thing in common: faith.

1. The woman with the issue of blood: "Your faith has made you whole." (Mark 5:34)

2. The blind men: "According to your faith be it unto you." (Matthew 9:29)

3. The centurion: "I have not found such great faith in all Israel." (Matthew 8:10)

None of these people had perfect lives or perfect theology—but they had faith.

They believed God could, they expected He would, and they acted like He already had. That kind of faith still draws miracles today.

Faith is not just belief—it's expectant belief. It says, "I know God is good, and I know He's going to show up for me." Faith reaches into the invisible and pulls out what God has already prepared.

"According to your faith let it be to you."

— Matthew 9:29

That means the level of blessing you walk in is often tied to the level of blessing you're expecting. This isn't prosperity hype—it's biblical truth. You become what you believe, and you attract what you consistently expect.

Spiritual Law: You Attract What You Expect

God created the world with laws—natural and spiritual. Just like the law of gravity works whether you believe it or not, the law of faith and expectation is always working.

"As a man thinks in his heart, so is he."

— Proverbs 23:7

If you constantly think, "I'm unlucky, overlooked, under attack,"—you are setting your expectation low and unconsciously resisting blessings. But when you wake up each day thinking, "God is with me. Favor surrounds me. I'm expecting blessings,"—you pull supernatural possibilities into your reality.

Expectation doesn't mean you ignore problems—it means you see God as bigger than your problems.

The Woman with the Issue of Blood

One of the most faith-filled examples of magnetic expectation is the woman with the issue of blood in Mark 5.

She had been bleeding for 12 years. She spent all her money on doctors and got worse. But one day, she heard about Jesus—and something in her heart leapt.

"For she said, 'If only I may touch His clothes, I shall be made well.'"

— Mark 5:28

She expected healing. She believed before it happened. And she acted on that faith. As soon as she touched Jesus' garment, power flowed into her, and she was instantly healed.

Jesus didn't say, "My clothes healed you," or "It was just your lucky day." No—He said:

"Daughter, your faith has made you well."

— Mark 5:34

Her faith, her expectation, her determination— attracted her healing. This woman didn't just get a miracle. She drew it out of Jesus through her faith.

Blessing Magnets Expect Daily Goodness

You don't need a crowd, a platform, or have everything together in your life to receive a blessing. You need expectation. And the great news is expectation is a choice. Every day, you can choose to expect God's goodness.

1. Expect divine appointments.

2. Expect financial favor.

3.   Expect answers to prayer.

4.   Expect wisdom for decisions.

5.   Expect doors to open that no man can shut.

"The Lord is good to those who wait for Him, to the soul who seeks Him." — Lamentations 3:25

Waiting in faith is expecting.

When you say, "I'm a blessing magnet," you're saying, "I live in holy expectation. I believe something good is coming my way today."

Prayer:

Father God,

Thank You for being faithful. Thank You that Your Word is full of promises for my life. I ask You to increase my faith and help me live with bold, joyful expectation. I reject fear, doubt, and unbelief. From this moment on, I expect Your favor, provision, and peace to follow me every day. I declare: "I am a blessing magnet."

In the name of Jesus, Amen.

Personal Reflection:

1.   What am I expecting most days—breakthrough or setbacks?

What has God promised me that I need to start expecting again?

2.   What would change in my life if I woke up every morning expecting a blessing?

Prophetic Confession:

"Father God, I choose today to expect Your best. I open my heart wide and believe You will bless me in ways I can't even imagine."

Speaking the Blessing

Chapter 3

Speaking the Blessing

"Death and life are in the power of the tongue, and those who love it will eat its fruit." — Proverbs 18:21 (NKJV)

You are not just a receiver of blessings—you also release blessings. One of the greatest truths you can ever learn is this: your mouth creates your world. What you consistently speak, you eventually see. You shape your life not just by your actions, but by your words.

If faith is the magnet for miracles, then your words are the switch that turns on the magnet. You cannot be a blessing magnet while constantly speaking doubt, fear, or lack. Blessing travels on the sound waves of faith.

The Power of Spoken Words

Words are not empty sound waves—they are spiritual containers. They either carry life or death, faith or fear, blessing or bondage. What you speak today becomes what you walk in tomorrow.

"By faith we understand that the worlds were framed by the word of God..." — Hebrews 11:3

God framed the universe with His Word. And through Christ, you now carry that same creative authority. You frame your own world by what you speak.

1.   Your words frame your relationships

2.   Your words shape your future

3.   Your words direct your emotions

4.   Your words define your atmosphere

You are never just "talking"—you are always creating or destroying.

Words Are Seeds

Jesus taught that the Word of God is like a seed (Luke 8:11). When you speak His Word, you are planting supernatural seeds in the soil of your life. Over time, with patience and faith, those seeds grow into harvests of blessings.

But when you speak words of fear, failure, or lack, you plant seeds that produce stress, stagnation, and strife.

"You will also declare a thing, and it will be established for you…" — Job 22:28

That's not just a motivational quote—it's a spiritual law. Your declarations become your reality.

Words Shape Belief and Break Limitation

Your words don't only affect your environment—they shape your inner man. When you speak truth, boldness, and faith, your mind is renewed and your spirit strengthened.

Even David, in the darkest moments of his life, didn't wait for someone else to lift him up:

"But David encouraged himself in the Lord his God."

— 1 Samuel 30:6

Jesus didn't just think the Word—He spoke it:

"It is written…" — Matthew 4:4

Your spoken words are not optional. They are your primary weapon in spiritual warfare. They bind, loose, shift atmospheres, and open doors.

Guard Your Mouth—Guard Your Future

"Set a guard, O Lord, over my mouth; keep watch over the door of my lips."

— Psalm 141:3

Many believers pray for blessings but speak against them in their daily language:

1.   "I'll never get out of this mess."

2.   "Things are always hard for me."

3.   guess it just wasn't meant to work."

These aren't just phrases—they're curses in disguise. You can't pray for rain and then speak drought. A blessing magnet must be intentional about what comes out of their mouth

You can't pray for rain and then speak drought. A blessing magnet must be intentional about what comes out of their mouth.

Biblical Example: The Shunammite Woman

In 2 Kings 4, the Shunammite woman was blessed with a miracle son. But one day, her son died unexpectedly. She didn't scream, panic, or speak death. She saddled her donkey and went to find the prophet Elisha.

When asked how things were going, she responded:

"It is well." — 2 Kings 4:23, 26

That wasn't denial—it was a declaration. She refused to speak death over a promise from God. Her faith-filled words drew resurrection power. Elisha prayed—and her son came back to life

How Spoken Words Work Spiritually

Spoken Word	Spiritual Effect
Speaking God's Word	Releases power and draws the blessing (Isaiah 55:11)
Speaking Faith	Attracts miracles and favor (Mark 11:23-24)
Speaking Negativity	Undermines progress and invites defeat (Proverbs 6:2)
Speaking in Agreement	Establishes what you declare (Job 22:28)
Declaring Identity	Reinforces your spiritual authority (Romans 10:10)

Living in God's Flow

To live as a blessing magnet is to live in rhythm with heaven—to move in sync with what God is doing, not just reacting to what you see. This is what it means to live in God's flow: a supernatural current of grace, timing, direction, and provision. In this flow, blessings don't need to be forced—they find you.

"In Him we live and move and have our being…"

— Acts 17:28

God's flow is not chaos. It's not rushing, forcing, or striving. It's a grace-guided stream that leads you through life with peace, purpose, and precision.

God's Flow Is Guided by the Spirit

"For all who are led by the Spirit of God are children of God." — Romans 8:14

When you are led by the Holy Spirit, you're no longer reacting out of fear or guessing your way forward. You are flowing with the One who sees the end from the beginning.

Living in God's flow means:

1. Being in the right place at the right time

2. Saying yes when He says go, and waiting when He says pause

3. Trusting His pace—even when it's slower than your preference

4. Letting Him redirect your plans without losing your peace

The flow of God is a current of divine timing. And when you're in it, you attract favor without manipulation and walk into opportunities without forcing them.

Biblical Example: Philip and the Ethiopian Eunuch

In Acts 8:26–40, Philip didn't try to create a ministry moment—he followed the flow.

"Then the Spirit said to Philip, 'Go near and overtake this chariot.'" — Acts 8:29

Because Philip flowed with the Spirit's leading, he ended up in the exact place where a man was ready to receive Christ. That one act of obedience led to the gospel reaching Ethiopia.

God's flow doesn't always make sense, but it always brings results.

Flow Keeps You from Forcing Things

Many people miss their blessings because they try to force outcomes instead of flowing in faith. But forcing leads to frustration, and flowing leads to fruitfulness.

When you're in God's flow:

1. You don't panic in the waiting—you rest in it.

2. You don't cling to doors God shuts—you walk to the ones He opens.

3. You stop chasing things and realize what's yours comes by grace.

This is how blessing becomes effortless. Not because life is perfect, but because you're aligned with the One who blesses.

Living in the Flow Means Trusting the Process

Even when the blessing is hidden, the flow keeps you moving forward. It keeps your spirit calm, your faith strong, and your ear tuned to heaven.

"The steps of a good man are ordered by the Lord..."
    — Psalm 37:23

Blessings come to those who walk—not race—in step with God.

How to Stay in God's Flow:

1. Daily surrender — Start each day saying: "Not my will, but Yours."

2. Listen for promptings — Pay attention to Holy Spirit nudges.

3. Let go of control — The flow doesn't work when you try to take over.

4. Trust His timing — The right blessing at the wrong time is still wrong.

5. Stay in motion — Don't freeze in fear. Keep flowing by faith.

Difference Between Force and Flow

Forcing It	**Flowing with God**
Striving and stressing	Surrender and peace
Pushing doors open	Walking through open doors
Driven by fear or pressure	Led by peace and confirmation
Result's in burnout	Result's in fruitfulness
Temporary satisfaction	Eternal impact

Prayer:

Father,

Teach me to live in Your divine rhythm. Help me to release control and move with Your Spirit. When You say go, I'll go. When You say wait, I'll trust. I surrender my own timing and plans so I can stay in Your flow. Let Your Spirit guide every step I take. In the name of Jesus, Amen.

Personal Reflection:

1.   Am I living in God's flow—or forcing my own way?

2.   Where is God inviting me to slow down, let go, or trust Him more?

3.   What would it look like to let God lead fully in this season?

Prophetic Confession:

"Lord, I choose to flow with You. I let go of control, and I trust Your perfect pace. Help me stay aligned with Your Spirit so that blessings will meet me at the right time..."

Positioned for Favor

Chapter 4

Positioned for Favor

"For You, O Lord, will bless the righteous; with favor You will surround him as with a shield."

— Psalm 5:12 (NKJV)

Favor is not random. It's not reserved for the lucky or the famous. God's favor is intentional, and He loves to pour it out — but He often pours it on those who are in position. Just like rain waters the ground that's uncovered, favor flows into the lives of those who are open, aligned, and expecting.

The truth is, you can be a blessing magnet and still miss out if you're not positioned properly. It's like having the right radio but being on the wrong frequency. Favor is already in the air — your job is to tune in.

What Does It Mean to Be Positioned?

To be "positioned for favor" means you're living in alignment with God's Word, walking by faith, and keeping your heart in a posture that welcomes God's blessing. It means you're not just chasing blessings — you're walking in step with the One who Blesses.

Think about Ruth. She wasn't born into the right family, and by natural standards, she had every reason to live in lack. But she positioned herself through:

1. Loyalty (she stayed with Naomi)

2. Obedience (she followed instructions)

3. Diligence (she worked in the field), and Humility (she didn't demand attention)

And what happened? She caught Boaz's eye, stepped into divine favor, and became part of Jesus' lineage. Ruth didn't chase favor — she was positioned for it.

Favor Finds the Aligned

One of the biggest keys to walking in favor is alignment — with God's will, with His timing, and with His values. Misalignment can block blessings. God won't bless what contradicts His Word. That's why it's so important to:

1. Forgive quickly

2. Obey His promptings

3. Stay connected to the right people

4. Honor Him with your choices

When you're in alignment, you don't have to force doors open. Favor opens them for you. It introduces you, promotes you, and places you in rooms you couldn't get into on your own.

Favor Has a Flow

God's favor is like a river. You don't have to make it — but you do have to step into it.

Here's how:

1. Stay in God's Presence – Favor is attracted to intimacy. The more time you spend with God, the more confident and clear you become. Moses found favor because he valued God's presence (Exodus 33:13–14).

2. Honor God's Principles – Tithing, integrity, generosity, humility — these are not just "good practices"; they are positioning tools.

3. Walk in Expectation – Expectation is the posture of faith. Expect favor in every area — relationships, opportunities, finances, and influence.

You can't always control your environment, but you can control your position.

Living in God's Flow

There is a rhythm to favor. God's flow is His divine timing, wisdom, and leading in motion — and it's often gentle but powerful. Favor flows best when you're not striving but trusting. When you're in God's flow, you:

1.   Stop forcing outcomes

2.   Stop comparing your path to others

3.   Start moving in step with God's Spirit

Psalm 1:1–3 paints the picture perfectly:

"Blessed is the man who walks not in the counsel of the ungodly… but his delight is in the law of the Lord, and in His law he meditates day and night. He shall be like a tree planted by the rivers of water, that brings forth its fruit in its season, whose leaf also shall not wither; and whatever he does shall prosper."

That's what it looks like to live in God's flow — planted, fruitful, and consistent. You're not dry or desperate; you're steady and supplied, because your roots go deep in God.

When you obey God and align with His Word, favor doesn't just trickle — it overtakes you.

"And all these blessings shall come upon you and overtake you, because you obey the voice of the Lord your God…" — Deuteronomy 28:2

That's the power of positioning. You don't have to chase the blessings; they come running after you.

Jesus modeled this perfectly. He said, "I only do what I see the Father doing" (John 5:19). He flowed with heaven's agenda. When you live in God's flow, things begin to happen without manipulation. Favor finds you as you follow His lead — even when it doesn't make immediate sense.

God's flow may not always be fast, but it is always fruitful. As you stay rooted in His Word, obedient to His voice, and surrendered to His plan, blessings will find you — in season, on time, and in abundance.

Avoiding Favor Blockers

Sometimes, people miss blessings not because God is not willing, but because their attitude, fear, or disobedience blocks the flow. Here are three common blockers:

1. Complaining – It focuses on lack and repels gratitude, which is the magnet for more.

2. Fear of Man – Trying to please everyone can cause you to miss God's instructions.

3. Pride – Favor elevates the humble (James 4:6). Pride is like a spiritual repellent to the blessings of God.

Check your heart regularly. Ask, "Lord, is there anything in me that's out of position?" His grace will gently realign you.

You Were Born Again to Walk in Favor

This is not about earning blessings — it's about receiving them. You are a child of the King. Favor is not a reward for perfection; it's a result of positioning. The Prodigal Son did not earn his father's blessings — he just came home and positioned himself as a son again.

You may not feel qualified. You may not feel worthy. But if you stay under God's covering, walk in obedience, and believe in His goodness, you will be surrounded with favor like a shield.

Prayer:

Father,

Thank You for Your divine favor. Help me walk in alignment with Your will. Show me any areas where I need to reposition my heart, my thoughts, or my actions. I trust Your flow. I surrender my timeline to You and choose to walk in step with Your Spirit. I believe that as I stay close to You, Your favor will surround, promote, and guide me into every blessing You have prepared. In the name of Jesus, amen.

Personal reflection:

1.) I realize that God's favor is not random – it flows when my heart and life are aligned with His Word.
2.) Today, I choose to position myself in faith, obedience, and expectation.
3.) I don't want to miss what God is pouring out – I want to be in the flow.

Prophetic Confession:

"I am positioned for favor. I walk in alignment with God's Word. I live in God's flow. I attract divine opportunities and strategic relationships. I do not chase blessings — blessings chase me. I am in the right place at the right time for God's best. I am a blessing magnet!"

Blessed to Be a Blessing

Chapter 5

Blessed to Be a Blessing

"I will bless you ... and you will be a blessing."
— Genesis 12:2 (NIV)

One of the greatest revelations you can ever receive is this: God blesses you not just for your own benefit, but so you can bless others. As a blessing magnet, your life is not a reservoir; it is a river. God's blessings are meant to flow to you and then through you.

The Abraham Principle

God's covenant with Abraham gives us the blueprint: "I will bless you ... and you will be a blessing." (Genesis 12:2). Notice the order: God blesses first, but there's an expectation that the blessing will continue its journey into the lives of others. This wasn't a one-time arrangement—it's a divine principle still in effect today. You are an heir of that same promise through Christ (Galatians 3:29). That means when God blesses your finances, your health, your relationships, your opportunities—it's not just about you. It's about who you're called to impact.

Receiving and Releasing Blessings

Blessings are never meant to stop with you—they are meant to flow through you. Scripture is filled with examples of people who received God's blessings and became channels of those blessings to others.

Joseph: From Pit to Palace to Provider

Joseph was sold into slavery and falsely imprisoned, yet God blessed him with wisdom, favor, and promotion. But it didn't stop there. When famine struck the land, it was Joseph's God-given position in Egypt that enabled him to feed nations—including the very family that betrayed him (Genesis 41–45).

"God sent me ahead of you to preserve for you a remnant on earth and to save your lives by a great deliverance." – Genesis 45:7 (NIV)

Lesson: God blessed Joseph so he could bless others in a time of need.

The Widow of Zarephath: A Little Becomes Overflow

In 1 Kings 17:8–16, a poor widow was down to her last meal during a severe famine. But when she obeyed the word of the prophet Elijah and gave her last bit of food, God miraculously multiplied her flour and oil. She and her household ate for many days.

"The jar of flour was not used up and the jug of oil did not run dry..." – 1 Kings 17:16 (NIV)

Lesson: Even a small act of generosity can release supernatural provision.

Jesus and the Loaves and Fish: Multiplying Blessing

In Matthew 14:13–21, a boy gave Jesus five loaves and two fish. Jesus blessed it, broke it, and distributed it—and it fed over five thousand people, with twelve baskets left over!

"They all ate and were satisfied..." – Matthew 14:20 (NIV)

Lesson: When you release what you have into God's hands, He multiplies it for the benefit of many.

God Trusts You with Blessings

God doesn't randomly pour out blessings. He's strategic. He blesses those He can trust to handle them wisely and share them generously. The more you grow in your willingness to bless others, the more God increases what He gives you. Why? Because He knows you will not hoard it—you will multiply it.

"Whoever can be trusted with very little can also be trusted with much..." – Luke 16:10 (NIV)

Are you trustworthy with what God has already given you? Gratitude leads to generosity, and generosity unlocks even more blessing.

Ways to Be a Blessing

Being a blessing means giving of your resources, giving your time, your encouragement, your attention, or your wisdom. Here are just a few ways you can activate this principle:

1.   Speak life. A kind word or prayer can change someone's day—or destiny

2.   Be generous. Support a cause. Help a family. Pay for someone's groceries. Let your money preach the gospel

3.   Share your story. Your testimony is a blessing someone else needs to hear

4.   Serve with joy. Volunteer. Support your church. Be an active vessel of love

When you live with this mindset, you become someone God can count on to reflect His heart.

The Boomerang of Blessing

Here's the beauty of God's economy: what you give never leaves your life—it just comes back multiplied.

"Give, and it will be given to you. A good measure, pressed down, shaken together and running over..."
    – Luke 6:38 (NIV)

This is not karma. It's Kingdom. As you bless others, you attract greater blessings. The more you give out of love, the more heaven pours into you.

Make Blessing Your Lifestyle

You were created to be a light in this world. And that light shines brightest when your life becomes a testimony of generosity, kindness, faith, and compassion. God's favor follows those who live to lift others.

Prayer:

"Lord, make me a blessing magnet—not just so I can be blessed, but so I can bless everyone You send my way. Use me to reflect Your goodness wherever I go."

Personal Reflection:

1.) God doesn't bless me just for my own comfort – He blesses me to be a channel of His goodness to others

2.) I want my life to reflect His generosity and compassion in every season

3.) Today, I open my hands and heart to receive freely and give freely

Living Every Day Like a Blessing Magnet

Chapter 6

Living Everyday Like a Blessing Magnet

Every day you wake up is an opportunity to walk in the supernatural favor of God. You're not waiting on blessings—you're walking in them. When you begin to live with deep gratitude and bold expectation, you'll start seeing blessings in places you once overlooked.

Being a blessing magnet isn't just something you say; it's a mindset, a lifestyle, and a reflection of what you truly believe about God's goodness.

1. Living with Gratitude and Bold Expectation

Gratitude shifts your atmosphere. Expectation activates the promises.

Many people live reactive lives—only praising God after blessings arrive. But a blessing magnet thanks God before the breakthrough because they know something good is always on the way.

"Sacrifice thank offerings to God, fulfill your vows to the Most High, and call on me in the day of trouble; I will deliver you, and you will honor me."

— Psalm 50:14–15

In the Old Testament, we see the example of Hannah, who, even before seeing her miracle child, prayed with faith. After pouring out her soul to God, she left the temple no longer sad (1 Samuel 1:18). Her attitude changed before her circumstances did—that's what bold expectation looks like.

The New Testament encourages this same posture:

"Let your gentleness be evident to all. The Lord is near. Do not be anxious about anything, but in every situation, by prayer and petition, with thanksgiving, present your requests to God."

— Philippians 4:5–6

Thanksgiving before the outcome is what opens the floodgates for blessings.

2. Expecting Everyday Miracles

If you only expect miracles during "spiritual highs," you'll miss the daily fingerprints of God. Blessing magnets see His hand in parking spots, unexpected texts of encouragement, divine delays, and quiet nudges.

In 2 Kings 4: 42–44, a man brings Elisha 20 loaves of barley bread to feed 100 men. Elisha commands it to be shared, and miraculously, "they ate and had some left over, according to the word of the Lord."

That wasn't a Red Sea moment—it was lunch. But God was in it.

In the New Testament, Jesus turns an ordinary fishing moment into a blessing explosion.

"Throw your net on the right side of the boat and you will find some." When they did, they were unable to haul the net in because of the large number of fish.

— John 21:6

That moment happened after Jesus had risen. Even after the Resurrection, Jesus still cared about their work, their needs, their daily lives.

Blessing magnets live in constant expectation of these "everyday miracles."

3. Testimonies from the Word and Real Life

Testimonies are God's receipts—evidence of His ability and willingness to bless.

Isaac sowed in a time of famine, and the Bible says:

"The man became rich, and his wealth continued to grow until he became very wealthy." — Genesis 26:13

He didn't wait for conditions to be perfect. He moved in faith, and the blessing followed.

1. Elizabeth, mother of John the Baptist, conceived in her old age.

"The Lord has done this for me... He has shown his favor and taken away my disgrace among the people."

— Luke 1:25

Her story reminds us that divine timing and divine blessing go hand-in-hand.

In modern times, people are seeing the same God show up:

2. A woman who had declared, "God delights in my prosperity," received a scholarship days before withdrawing from her degree program.

3. A young man wrote "I am a blessing magnet" on his mirror. He got three unexpected job offers in one week.

4. A couple in debt began praying over their finances and sowing faithfully. Within six months, they were debt-free and promoted.

Testimonies are prophetic in nature—what God did for them; He can do for you.

4. Activate Your Faith Daily

You can't live like a blessing magnet only on Sundays. Faith must be daily, practical, and persistent.

Speak Faith

"The Sovereign Lord has given me a well-instructed tongue, to know the word that sustains the weary."

— Isaiah 50:4

Your words should sustain your spirit and attract blessings. Speak life over your day, your family, your health, and your finances. What you confess, you attract.

Walk with Faith

"For we live by faith, not by sight."

— 2 Corinthians 5:7

Don't wait until circumstances look perfect to believe. Step forward with the confidence that God is going ahead of you.

Pray Faith

"But you, dear friends, by building yourselves up in your most holy faith and praying in the Holy Spirit..."

— Jude 1:20

Prayer is how you charge your spirit and align your mind with heaven's reality. A blessing magnet stays plugged in through consistent, faith-filled prayer.

5. Be a Blessing Everywhere You Go

You were never meant to be a cul-de-sac for blessings—you're a channel. When you become a blessing to others, God multiplies them back to you.

"The generous will themselves be blessed, for they share their food with the poor."

— Proverbs 22:9

"Each of you should use whatever gift you have received to serve others, as faithful stewards of God's grace in its various forms."

— 1 Peter 4:10

When you make room for others to be blessed through you, heaven makes room for more blessings to flow to you.

Blessings Are Looking for You

You're not chasing blessings—they're chasing you.

"All these blessings will come on you and accompany you if you obey the Lord your God."

— Deuteronomy 28:2

That means blessings are assigned to follow you around. When you wake up, get dressed, go to work, go shopping—you're a moving magnet for favor, open doors, divine ideas, and heavenly surprises.

Live every day knowing:

God has a blessing scheduled for today.

Heaven is already working in your favor.

You are aligned with the promises of the Most High.

Prayer:

Lord, help me to wake up each day with bold expectation and a thankful heart. Teach me to recognize Your hand in the little and the big things. Let my life reflect Your favor and draw others to Your goodness.

Personal Reflection:

1.) Every day is an opportunity to expect God's goodness and walk in His favor.

2.) Being a blessing magnet means staying in faith, even when I don't see it yet—I know God is working.

Prophetic Confession

"Today, I live like a blessing magnet. I speak with boldness, walk in faith, and expect miracles. God's favor surrounds me like a shield. I am blessed to be a blessing, and every need is met. I attract divine help, daily provision, and heavenly opportunities—because I believe and receive, in the name of Jesus. Amen."

Prayer Power of a

Blessing Magnet

Chapter 7

Prayer Power of a Blessing Magnet

Blessing Starts in the Secret Place

Every blessing that manifests in the visible world begins in the invisible place of prayer. Before the door opens, before the miracle unfolds, and before the opportunity appears — a Blessing Magnet has already been praying. They don't chase blessings — they commune with the One who blesses.

Prayer is not a ritual for religious people; it is the lifeline for those who walk in divine favor. A Blessing Magnet doesn't just pray when there's a problem — they live in a constant rhythm of fellowship with God, releasing Heaven into their everyday lives.

"The blessing of the Lord brings wealth, without painful toil for it."

— Proverbs 10:22 (NIV)

Prayer is not begging. It's releasing what already belongs to you through faith and spiritual authority. A Blessing Magnet doesn't just pray when things go wrong — they constantly invite His favor into every area of their lives.

Prayers That Attract Blessing

Blessing Magnets pray differently. Their prayers are not rooted in fear, but in faith. They speak life, not lack. They pray God's Word, not their worry. Their hearts are filled with gratitude, not grumbling.

Prayer Positions You for the Blessing

When you live a lifestyle of prayer, you stay in a position to receive. You don't have to manipulate or compete. You don't have to force doors open. Instead, prayer becomes the steering wheel of your day — guiding you into divine timing, divine connections, and divine protection.

"You will call on me and come and pray to me, and I will listen to you."

— Jeremiah 29:12 (NIV)

Prayer prepares your heart so that when the blessing comes, you'll be ready and not be prideful, but humble… not distracted, but discerning… not just receiving, but also releasing and becoming a channel of blessing to others!

Blessing Magnets Who Prayed

1. Jabez — A Prayer That Rewrote His Story

Jabez was born into pain, but he refused to let that define his destiny. Instead of accepting a cursed identity, he prayed a bold, faith-filled prayer:

"Oh, that You would bless me indeed, and enlarge my territory, that Your hand would be with me, and that You would keep me from evil…"

— 1 Chronicles 4:10 (NKJV)

And what happened next? "So, God granted him what he requested."

Jabez prayed like a Blessing Magnet — he did not beg God. He believed God. He asked with boldness and expected God's hand to move. His prayer changed the trajectory of his life.

2. Hannah — A Prayer That Birthed a Prophet

Hannah was barren, ridiculed, and deeply distressed. Instead of becoming bitter, she became better by praying like a warrior. She poured out her soul to God in the temple, asking not only for a child, but promising to dedicate him back to the Lord.

"In her deep anguish Hannah prayed to the Lord, weeping bitterly."

— 1 Samuel 1:10 (NIV)

Her son Samuel became one of the greatest prophets in Israel's history. Hannah's prayer wasn't selfish — it was surrendered. And because of that, it attracted not just a blessing for her, but a blessing for a nation.

3. Elijah — A Prayer That Brought Rain

After three and a half years of drought, Elijah climbed to the top of Mount Carmel and prayed for rain. There were no clouds in sight. But he sent his servant to check the sky seven times — because Elijah knew God would answer.

"Elijah climbed to the top of Carmel, bent down to the ground and put his face between his knees."

— 1 Kings 18:42 (NIV)

On the seventh time, a small cloud appeared — and soon, the skies opened. Elijah's prayer broke the drought. His persistent faith attracted the rain of blessing.

The Prayer Life of a Blessing Magnet

Blessing Magnets don't pray out of desperation — they pray out of expectation. They declare what God says, even when they don't see it yet. They understand that prayer is not just communication — it's activation.

Their prayers:

- Align with God's Word
- Are fueled by faith, not fear
- Release blessing into their lives and others'

"You will also declare a thing, and it will be established for you; so light will shine on your ways."

— Job 22:28 (NKJV)

Daily Prayer Declaration of a Blessing Magnet

Here's a declaration you can speak aloud to activate your faith and attract Heaven's provision:

Prayer:

"Father, I thank You that I am a magnet for Your blessings. I walk in divine favor and supernatural overflow. Let Your hand be upon me today — for wisdom, provision, and purpose. I declare that blessings are overtaking me, not for my comfort alone, but so I can be a blessing to others. In the name of Jesus, Amen."

Personal Reflection:

1.) What have your prayers sounded like lately — are they full of faith or fear?
2.) How can you begin praying the promises of God instead of the problems?
3.) Who can you begin praying for, so that you become a blessing even before you receive one?

Confession Scriptures for Prayer-Driven Blessing Magnets

Psalm 5:12 (NIV) — "Surely, Lord, you bless the righteous; you surround them with your favor as with a shield."

Mark 11:24 (NLT) — "I tell you, you can pray for anything, and if you believe that you've received it, it will be yours."

Ephesians 3:20 (NKJV) — "Now to Him who is able to do exceedingly abundantly above all that we ask or think, according to the power that works in us…

Be Grateful

Chapter 8

Be Grateful

Gratitude Is a Magnet for Blessings

Gratitude is not just polite — it's powerful. In the Kingdom of God, gratitude is a force that attracts more of what Heaven wants to release in your life. A Blessing Magnet is not someone who waits until the miracle arrives to give God thanks. No — they give thanks in advance. They praise before they see the provision. They rejoice before the breakthrough comes. Gratitude is how you say to God, "I trust You, even before I see it." That kind of faith moves Heaven.

Gratitude Is Not a Feeling — It's a Faith Response

Gratitude doesn't depend on how you feel — it depends on what you believe.

If you wait to feel thankful before giving thanks, you'll miss many opportunities to unlock God's blessing. Faith gives thanks before the breakthrough. Gratitude is a decision to trust God's character, not your circumstances.

"Through Him then let us continually offer up a sacrifice of praise to God..." — Hebrews 13:15(ESV)

Sometimes gratitude is a sacrifice — you offer it when it costs you. That's when it carries the most power.

Give Thanks Regardless

"Give thanks in all circumstances; for this is God's will for you in Christ Jesus."

> — 1 Thessalonians 5:18 (NIV)

"Enter His gates with thanksgiving and His courts with praise; give thanks to Him and praise His name."

> — Psalm 100:4 (NIV)

"Abraham never wavered in believing God's promise… He grew strong in faith as he gave glory to God."

> — Romans 4:20 (NLT)

Gratitude opens the gate to the presence of God. Praise makes room for His blessings to flow.

Jesus and the Multiplication of Bread (John 6:11)

When Jesus fed the five thousand, He didn't complain about the little that was available. He took the five loaves and two fish — and gave thanks. That act of gratitude triggered multiplication. The miracle didn't happen after they got more food — it happened when He gave thanks for what they had and for what they were expecting. Thanksgiving is the spiritual trigger for supernatural increase.

Gratitude Is a Weapon of Faith

Grateful people live with an open heaven. They are not blind to their problems — they just choose to keep their eyes on God's faithfulness.

When others panic, they praise. When others shrink back, they speak up. Gratitude is their warfare. Praise is their posture.

Blessing Magnets live in the present, but they praise like the promise has already come.

"I will bless the Lord at all times; His praise shall continually be in my mouth." — Psalm 34:1 (KJV)

What Did Jesus Likely Say in Hebrew when He gave thanks before the bread and fish multiplied?

He would have spoken a Jewish blessing called a "Berakhah", and for bread, the traditional blessing in Hebrew: בָּרוּךְ אַתָּה יְיָ אֱלֹהֵינוּ מֶלֶךְ הָעוֹלָם הַמּוֹצִיא לֶחֶם מִן הָאָרֶץ It is pronounced: Baruch atah Adonai Eloheinu *Melech ha'olam, hamotzi lechem min ha'aretz.*

Translation in English: "Blessed are You, O Lord our God, King of the universe, who brings forth bread from the earth."

Why Complaining Blocks the Flow

The Israelites saw miracle after miracle, but their constant complaining kept them wandering in circles. They received blessings — but never entered into God's best. Why? Because murmuring is ingratitude and a sign of mistrust.

You can't attract blessings if your words are full of bitterness. You can't walk in overflow with a grumbling heart. But when you choose gratitude, even in lack or confusion, you open the door for miracles.

Gratitude Is the Will of God

Notice it doesn't say give thanks for all things — it says give thanks in all things. That means you can thank God in the storm, in the waiting, in the stretching, and in the blessing. This is how we align ourselves with the will of God — by offering thanksgiving regardless of the situation.

Gratitude Ushers You into God's Presence

"In Your presence there is fullness of joy; at Your right hand are pleasures forevermore." — Psalm 16:11 (ESV)

Thanksgiving is how we access the courts of Heaven. When you give thanks, you're not just practicing good manners — you're stepping into the presence of God. Blessings flow from His presence.

Abraham Praised in Faith

"He did not waver at the promise of God through unbelief, but was strengthened in faith, giving glory to God." — Romans 4:20 (NKJV)

Even before Isaac was born, Abraham praised God for the promise. He had no physical proof, but his praise was the proof of his faith. His gratitude honored God and drew the miracle into reality.

Why Gratitude Protects You from Settling

"Nor should we grumble, as some of them did—and were killed by the destroying angel." — 1 Corinthians 10:10 (NLT)

Murmuring focuses on what's missing. Thanksgiving magnifies what's coming. Gratitude keeps you moving toward the Promised Land instead of getting stuck in the wilderness.

Gratitude is the Language of the Faithful

"I will bless the Lord at all times; His praise shall continually be in my mouth." — Psalm 34:1 (KJV) Blessing Magnets speak with thankful tongues. Even when circumstances are hard, their confession is: "God is good, and He is faithful." They don't allow their mouths to cancel what their faith is believing for.

The Meaning of Gratitude in Hebrew and Greek

Hebrew Word for Gratitude: "Yadah" (יָדָה)

The primary Hebrew word often translated as thanks or thanksgiving is "Yadah". It literally means "to throw out the hands," or "to lift the hands in praise and confession."

"I will give thanks (yadah) to You, Lord, with all my heart; I will tell of all Your wonderful deeds." — Psalm 9:1 (NIV)

"Yadah" teaches us that gratitude is not just an inward feeling — it's something we show, speak, and release with boldness.

- Greek Word for Gratitude: "Eucharisteo" (εὐχαριστέω)
- "Eu" = good or well
- "Charis" = grace
- "Eucharisteo" literally means: to acknowledge the goodness of grace.

"Give thanks (eucharisteo) in all circumstances; for this is God's will for you in Christ Jesus."

— 1 Thessalonians 5:18 (NIV)

It's a deep recognition of God's undeserved favor and active goodness in your life. When Jesus gave thanks before feeding the five thousand (John 6:11), the word used is "eucharisteo."

Spiritual Insight

Biblical gratitude is not shallow. It's not just good manners — it's deep, spiritual insight that says:

- "God has been good to me" (Yadah — so I will praise Him).

- "God's grace is always working for me" (Eucharisteo — so I will give thanks).

Gratitude is how faith responds to grace. And Blessing Magnets make that response daily.

Prayer

Father, thank You — not just for what You have done, but for what You are doing even now. I choose to live with a thankful heart, even in the waiting. I praise You before the miracle comes, because I know You are faithful. Teach me to resist complaining and to rejoice in every season. In Jesus' name, Amen.

Reflection

1. What is one area of your life you've been silent about — where you can now begin to give thanks in advance?

2. How does gratitude affect your outlook and attitude each day?

3. What steps can you take to make thanksgiving part of your daily lifestyle?

Faith Confession

I live with a grateful heart.

I thank God in all things and for all things.

My praise is powerful — it invites God's favor.

I speak thanksgiving before I see the breakthrough.
I am a Blessing Magnet, and gratitude is my constant song.

Blessing Magnet
Daily Checklist

Blessing Magnet Daily Checklist

Version 1: Printable Page

Use this checklist every day to align your thoughts, words, and actions with God's blessing over your life. Print and post it on your mirror, desk, or inside your journal.

START YOUR DAY IN ALIGNMENT

- ☐ I thanked God for something specific today.
- ☐ I declared I am blessed and highly favored.
- ☐ I expected something good to happen today.

SPEAK LIFE & SCRIPTURE

- ☐ I spoke a faith-filled declaration over my life.
- ☐ I confessed God's promises, not my problems.
- ☐ I spoke what I want to see, not just what I see.

ACTIVATE FAITH THROUGH PRAYER

- ☐ I prayed with expectation, not routine.
- ☐ I asked God for direction, provision, or favor.
- ☐ I paused to listen for His voice.

WATCH FOR DAILY MIRACLES

- ☐ I noticed small blessings today.
- ☐ I recorded a testimony or answered prayer.
- ☐ I gave God glory in the moment.

BE A BLESSING TO OTHERS

- ☐ I encouraged someone today.
- ☐ I gave or served in some way.
- ☐ I released blessing without expecting return.

END-OF-DAY REFLECTION

- ☐ What unexpected, good thing happened today?
- ☐ Where did I see God's hand?
- ☐ What can I believe God for tomorrow?

DECLARE THIS

"I am a blessing magnet. I expect miracles, walk in favor, and live under an open heaven. Blessings come to me and flow through me, every day."

Version 2: Journal Insert

Blessing Magnet Reflection Journal

Day: _____

✔ Thanking God for:

_____

✔ Declaring: "I am blessed because

_____"

✔ Expecting good things by believing God for:

_____

My faith-filled declaration today:

"_____

_____"

I noticed God's hand today when:

_____

_____

_____

I blessed someone by:

☐ Encouraging ☐ Giving ☐ Praying ☐ Serving

Other:

_____

Testimony or answered prayer I saw today:

_____

_____

What I'm believing God for tomorrow:

_____

Declaration of the Day:

"I attract divine favor, peace, and provision. I walk in blessings and carry blessings. I'm a blessing magnet—today, tomorrow, and always."

POSTSCRIPT

If this book has inspired, encouraged, or challenged you in any way, we would love to hear your story. Your testimony is powerful — not only does it bless and encourage me as the author, but it also becomes a light for others who may be walking a similar journey. Whether this book stirred your faith, brought clarity to your calling, or ignited a deeper hunger within you for the things of God, your testimony matters. Please email us at: pa@cityrevive.org or go@cityrevive.org

You can send a written letter or an email to let us know how this book has touched your heart, shifted your perspective, or produced fruit in your life. Every testimony is a reminder that God's Word never returns void. Your words might be exactly what someone else needs to read one day.

CONNECT

Stay connected with us beyond the pages of this book! We invite you to follow us on Facebook, Threads, and Instagram for encouragement, updates, and behind-the-scenes glimpses of what God is doing through this ministry. Be sure to subscribe to our YouTube channel, where you'll find powerful teachings, testimonies, and uplifting content designed to strengthen your walk with Christ.

To learn more about our vision, mission, and how you can be part of what God is building, visit our website at cityrevive.org. Visit wordnspirit.tv to watch life-changing messages that will equip and empower you to live in the fullness of God's Spirit. We're honored to walk this journey with you!

CONNECT

Facebook: facebook.com/drstevembua

Instagram: @drstevembua

TikTok: @drstevembua

Youtube: @cityrevive

Website: cityrevive.org

To Give: cityrevive.org/give

Video On Demand: wordnspirit.tv

About the Author

About the Author

Dr. Steve Mbua is a passionate Bible teacher, author, and faith-building charismatic leader with a calling to help believers live in the fullness of God's promises. Known for his prophetic insight and empowering messages, Dr. Mbua equips people around the world to walk in faith, favor, and supernatural breakthrough. He is the author of several books including I'm a Blessing Magnet, a transformative guide designed to stir up bold expectation and activate the blessing of God in everyday life.

Dr. Mbua and his wife Rev. Lydienne Mbua are the founders and lead ministers of City Revival Church in Salado, Texas where they teach people how to align with Heaven and impact their world with the power of God's Word

Notes

<u>Notes</u>

<u>Notes</u>

Notes

Made in the USA
Columbia, SC
20 June 2025

59554720R00048